P9-CQJ-494

0 00 30 0284575 2

RECEIVED

FEB 1 4 2008

By_____

Levers

by Michael Dahl

Bridgestone Books
an Imprint of Capstone Press

Bridgestone Books are published by Capstone Press
818 North Willow Street, Mankato, Minnesota 56001
Copyright © 1996 by Capstone Press
Printed in the United States of America

Library of Congress Cataloging-in-Publication Data
Dahl, Michael S.
    Levers/by Michael S. Dahl
    p. cm. -- (Early reader science. Simple machines)
    Includes bibliographical references and index.
    Summary: Describes many different kinds, uses, and benefits of levers.
    ISBN 1-56065-444-9
    1. Levers--Juvenile literature. [1. Levers.] I. Title. II. Series
TJ147.D323 1996
621.8'11--dc20

                                        96-27770
                                          CIP
                                          AC

Photo credits
FPG/Michael Krasowitz, 20. International Stock/Elliot Smith, 14. Stokka
Productions, cover. Unicorn/Betts Anderson-Lohman, 8, 18; Dennis
Thompson, 12. Visuals Unlimited/C.E. Arnett, 6; Nancy L. Cushing, 10; J.
Daly, 4; Bernd Wittich, 16

Table of Contents

Words in **boldface** type in the text are defined in the
Words to Know section in the back of this book.

Machines

Machines are any **tools** that help people do work. A lever is a machine. A bottle opener is an example of a lever.

Levers

Every lever is made of a **bar** and a **fulcrum**. The bar is the part of the lever that moves and turns. The fulcrum is the point that does not move. A teeter-totter is a kind of lever.

Lifting a Load

A pencil and a roll of paper towels can work together as a lever to lift a book. The pencil is the bar and the roll of paper towels is the fulcrum. The book is the lever's **load**. The lever makes it easier to lift the load.

Levers in Action

The teeter-totter's fulcrum is in the very center of the bar. The fulcrum lets one child easily lift another child on a teeter-totter. Without the lever, the children could not lift each other.

First-Class Levers

Hammers and teeter-totters are both levers. Each has the fulcrum placed somewhere between the **effort** and the load. When a lever has its fulcrum in the middle, it is called a first-class lever.

Second-Class Levers

A wheelbarrow is another kind of lever. The wheelbarrow's fulcrum is the wheel. The load is in the middle, between the fulcrum and the worker. This makes the wheelbarrow a second-class lever.

Third-Class Levers

A broom is a lever. The fulcrum is where the hand grips the broom at the top. The load is on the floor where the broom is sweeping dust or dirt. The work is done by the hand in the middle of the broom. It is a third-class lever when the work is done between the fulcrum and the load.

Two or More Levers Together

The handle of a nail clippers is a lever that pushes the blades together. The blades are another lever system. When two or more levers work together, we call them **combination levers**.

Levers Are Everywhere

People use levers every day to help them with their work. Levers make work and play easier. A world without levers would have no baseball bats, hockey sticks, fishing poles, or pianos.

Hands On: Make Your Own Lever

With a lever, you can lift more rocks than you think you can.

What You Need

- A bag with handles
- Several rocks
- Strong string
- A broom handle
- A table

What You Do

1. Put the rocks in the bag. Feel how heavy it is.
2. Tie one end of the string around the bag's handles.
3. Tie the other end of the string around the middle of the broom handle.
4. Rest one end of the broom handle on the table.
5. Lift the other end of the broom handle, pulling the bag of rocks off the floor.

The bag of rocks feels lighter than it did before. The lever has made your work easier. The fulcrum of your lever is the table. The bag of rocks is your load. The load is between the fulcrum and the worker, so it is a second-class lever.

Words to Know

bar—the stiff part of a lever that moves and turns

combination levers—levers that work together toward the same goal

effort—the energy a person does to a machine

fulcrum—the part of the lever that stays in one place

load—whatever the lever moves or lifts

tool—anything a person uses to get a job done

Read More

Ardley, Neil. *The Science Book of Machines*. New York: Harcourt Brace Jovanovich, 1992.

Berenstain, Stan and Jan. *The Berenstain Bears' Science Fair*. New York: Random House, 1977.

VanCleave, Janice. *Janice VanCleave's Machines*. New York: John Wiley & Sons, 1993.

VanCleave, Janice. *Physics for Every Kid*. New York: John Wiley & Sons, 1991.

Index